WOULD Y

GAME RULES

1. Read every question out loud.
2. All ladies need to give their answer.
3. If someone refuses to share their answer - there is a challenge instead!*

HAVE FUN, LADIES!

*Remeber - safety first! Have fun but you need to feel comfortable and safe with what you`re doing

WOULD YOU RATHER...

have sex under
the shower

or...

on the kitchen
table??

CHALLENGE!

grab a banana and fake a blowjob for 30 seconds

WOULD YOU RATHER...

have unlimited
sex

or...

unlimited
money??

CHALLENGE!

twerk it!
for 30 seconds

WOULD YOU RATHER...

accidentally send
a dirty text to
your boss

or...

to your mom??

CHALLENGE!

drink one SOUR shot!

WOULD YOU RATHER...

cheat with your
best friend

or...

cheat with your
ex??

CHALLENGE!

tell everybody when and where was the last time you had sex?

WOULD YOU RATHER...

be a virgin
forever

or...

have sex with your
brother/sister one
time??

CHALLENGE!

tell us your worse date that ended with sex

WOULD YOU RATHER...

have oral sex

or...

anal sex only??

CHALLENGE!

drink one shot
with MILK!

WOULD YOU RATHER...

fuck an ugly genius

or...

a hot idiot??

CHALLENGE!

give someone a
lap dance now!
for 30 seconds

WOULD YOU RATHER...

fuck your boss

or...

fuck a total
stranger??

CHALLENGE!

say "hey gorgeus" to the first guy you see when you go out tonight!

WOULD YOU RATHER...

be caught in the
act by a cop

or...

by your parents??

CHALLENGE!

tell us what's
your secret
talent in bed?

WOULD YOU RATHER...

walk in on your best friend naked

or...

have your best friend walk in on you naked??

CHALLENGE!

scroll through your contact list with closed eyes - stop - say one mean thing about the person you landed on

WOULD YOU RATHER...

walk in on your parents having sex

or...

have them walk in on you??

CHALLENGE!

call a phone sex line and pretend that you have an apple pie fetish

WOULD YOU RATHER...

have a fairytale
wedding

or...

have a fairytale
honeymoon??

CHALLENGE!

tell us the worst thing your ex did in bed

WOULD YOU RATHER...

get caught
cheating

or...

catch your boo
cheating??

CHALLENGE!

point out a co-player in the room you would do it with right now

WOULD YOU RATHER...

have your man cheat on
you with a different
girl every month for a year

or...

cheat on you with
one person for
twelve months??

CHALLENGE!

name two sexual

things you're

not into

WOULD YOU RATHER...

have great foreplay
but bad sex

or...

lousy foreplay but
great sex??

CHALLENGE!

use the wrong bathroom
in a bar tonight!

WOULD YOU RATHER...

talk dirty during sex

or...

be completely mute
while doing it?

CHALLENGE!

draw your
vagina

WOULD YOU RATHER...

shave your partner's bush

or...

have them shave your pussy??

CHALLENGE!

lick someone's ear!

WOULD YOU RATHER...

have a threesome with
someone you know

or...

invite a complete
stranger??

CHALLENGE!

tell us your sex toys collection! DETAILS!

WOULD YOU RATHER...

give head to your boss

or...

give head to a
stranger??

CHALLENGE!

drink two shots in a row!

WOULD YOU RATHER...

be an escort

or...

a porn star??

CHALLENGE!

get a guy to autograph your chest!

WOULD YOU RATHER...

pay for sex

or...

get paid for it??

CHALLENGE!

go to the neighbours and ask them for a spare condom!

WOULD YOU RATHER...

be incredibly rich

or...

incredibly good-
looking??

CHALLENGE!

spank someone
really nice and
hard

WOULD YOU RATHER...

give up showering

or...

brushing your teeth for a whole week??

CHALLENGE!

name a famous celebrity you have fantasized about

WOULD YOU RATHER...

be attractive but not
so intelligent

or...

unattractive but
incredibly smart??

CHALLENGE!

show us the last tex you got from your man or your date

WOULD YOU RATHER...

accidentaly pocket-dial your <u>mom</u>

or...

your <u>dad</u> and have her/him listen to you having sex??

CHALLENGE!

give us your
sexy, dirty talk -
three sentences!

WOULD YOU RATHER...

your partner proposed
to you after one week

or...

after 10 years??

CHALLENGE!

name two public
places you had
sex in

WOULD YOU RATHER...

be twice as happy

or...

twice as wise??

CHALLENGE!

close your eyes and send a blind text to a random person from your contact list

WOULD YOU RATHER...

have awesome sex
that lasts 3 minutes

or...

boring sex that lasts
45 minutes (for the
rest of your life)??

CHALLENGE!

show everybody
your bra!

WOULD YOU RATHER...

always go out with
your husband

or...

always go out by
yourself??

CHALLENGE!

when you go out tonight, buy the saddest guy in the bar a drink

WOULD YOU RATHER...

go down on your man

or...

have him go down on you??

CHALLENGE!

say a nice thing to
every single
person in the room

WOULD YOU RATHER...

have your toes
sucked

or...

your armpit licked
during sex??

CHALLENGE!

take a body shot!
you may choose the
person

WOULD YOU RATHER...

be a lousy kisser

or...

give lousy blow
jobs??

CHALLENGE!

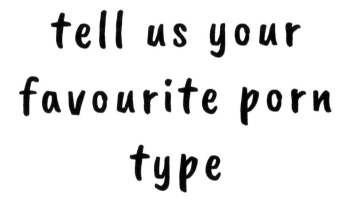

tell us your
favourite porn
type

Manufactured by Amazon.ca
Bolton, ON

16102236R00037